DREAM JOBS IN
HUMAN
SERVICES

HELEN MASON

CRABTREE
PUBLISHING COMPANY
WWW.CRABTREEBOOKS.COM

CUTTING-EDGE CAREERS IN TECHNICAL EDUCATION

Author:
Helen Mason

Series research and development:
Reagan Miller

Editorial director:
Kathy Middleton

Editor:
Petrice Custance

Proofreader:
Lorna Notsch

Design, photo research, and prepress:
Katherine Berti

Print and production coordinator:
Katherine Berti

Photographs:
Alamy
  BSIP SA: p. 25 (top)
  PG Arphexad: p. 17 (bottom left)
FEMA
  News Photo: p. 5 (top)
iStockphoto
  andresr: p. 16 (bottom)
  Gerri Medley: p. 29 (top right)
  Ossiridian: p. 29 (bottom left)
Shutterstock
  Alf Ribeiro: p. 25 (bottom)
  Alina R: p. 28 (bottom)
  dcwcreations: p. 27 (top left)
  DW labs Incorporated:
  p. 12 (bottom left)

michelmond: p. 5 (center)
muhammad afzan bin awang:
  p. 10 (bottom)
Pierre-Yves Babelon: p. 7 (top right)
Pamela Brick: p. 5 (bottom)
Ruzely Abdullah: front cover
  (center inset)
Veran36: p. 9 (bottom right)
Yulia Reznikov: p. 27 (magazine inset)
ThinkstockPhotos
  p. 18 (top), 22 (top), 23 (bottom)
Wikimedia
  Helioprmedia: p. 7 (bottom, inset)
All other images by Shutterstock

Library and Archives Canada Cataloguing in Publication

Mason, Helen, 1950-, author
    Dream jobs in human services / Helen Mason.
(Cutting-edge careers in technical education)
Includes index.
Issued in print and electronic formats.
ISBN 978-0-7787-4441-2 (hardcover).--
ISBN 978-0-7787-4452-8 (softcover).--
ISBN 978-1-4271-2032-8 (HTML)
    1. Social service--Vocational guidance--Juvenile literature. 2. Social
workers--Training of--Juvenile literature. 3. Human services--Vocational
guidance--Juvenile literature. 4. Human services personnel--Training of--
Juvenile literature. 5. Customer services--Vocational guidance--Juvenile
literature. 6. Customer services--Employees--Training of--Juvenile
literature. I. Title.
HV10.5.M376 2018   j361.3'2   C2018-900266-2
                                            C2018-900267-0

Library of Congress Cataloging-in-Publication Data

Names: Mason, Helen, 1950- author.
Title: Dream jobs in human services / Helen Mason.
Description: New York : Crabtree Publishing Company, [2018] |
    Series: Cutting-edge careers in technical education | Includes index.
Identifiers: LCCN 2018004039 (print) | LCCN 2018007177 (ebook) |
    ISBN 9781427120328 (Electronic) |
    ISBN 9780778744412 (hardcover : alk. paper) |
    ISBN 9780778744528 (pbk. : alk. paper)
Subjects: LCSH: Human services--Vocational guidance--Juvenile literature. |
    Service industries--Vocational guidance--Juvenile literature.
Classification: LCC HV10.5 (ebook) | LCC HV10.5 .M375 2018 (print) | DDC
    361.0023--dc23
LC record available at https://lccn.loc.gov/2018004039

Crabtree Publishing Company
www.crabtreebooks.com   1-800-387-7650

Printed in the U.S.A./052018/CG20180309

Published in Canada
Crabtree Publishing
616 Welland Ave.
St. Catharines, Ontario
L2M 5V6

Published in the United States
Crabtree Publishing
PMB 59051
350 Fifth Avenue, 59th Floor
New York, New York 10118

Published in the United Kingdom
Crabtree Publishing
Maritime House
Basin Road North, Hove
BN41 1WR

Published in Australia
Crabtree Publishing
3 Charles Street
Coburg North
VIC 3058

CONTENTS

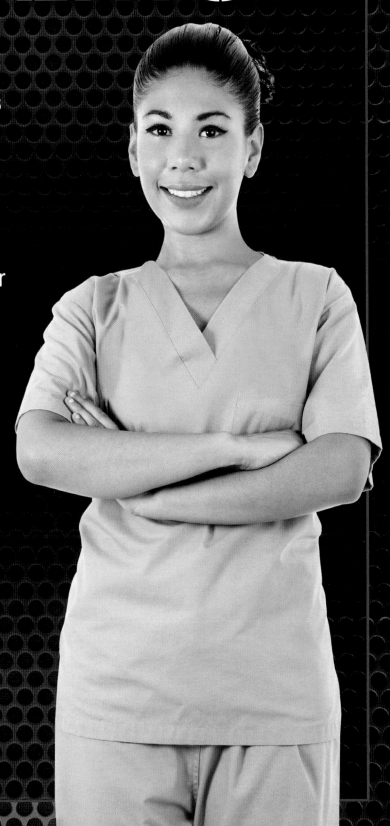

4   Jobs in Career and Technical Education

6   Jobs in Human Services

8   Preschool Teacher

10   Teacher Assistant

12   Art Therapist

14   Mental Health Counselor

16   Physical Therapist Assistant

18   Child and Youth Worker

20   Esthetician

22   Funeral Attendant

24   In-Home Health Aide

26   Credit Counselor

28   Special Events Coordinator

30   Learning More

31   Glossary

32   Index

JOBS IN CAREER AND TECHNICAL EDUCATION

Do you like variety? Do you want to wake up each morning looking forward to what the day will bring? Are you looking for a job that suits both your interests and your personality? Then Career and Technical Education is the answer for you.

Career and Technical Education (CTE) programs combine academic studies, such as math and science, with valuable hands-on training. CTE students develop job-specific skills that are in high demand by employers. CTE programs are divided into 16 career clusters. Some examples of these career clusters are Architecture and Construction, Human Services, Information Technology, and Arts and Communications.

Each CTE career cluster is divided into job pathways. Each job pathway is a grouping of jobs that require similar interests and paths of study. For example, in the Arts and Communications cluster, the Visual Arts pathway includes such jobs as photographer and graphic designer, while the Journalism and Broadcasting pathway includes jobs such as journalist and radio and television announcer.

Reporters warn the public when threatening storms are approaching.

BREAKING NEWS

LIVE NEWS

HURRICANE SLAMS COAST

Rainfall of 2 to 3 inches

When a disaster such as a hurricane occurs, emergency crews are there to help.

WHY CTE?

There's a wide variety of career choices in CTE. They include everything from conducting tours up **Mount Everest** to planning the **pyrotechnics** for an exciting pop concert!

Employers need people who embrace challenge. Such challenges can involve figuring out how an engine works or how to market a new gadget. Students who enjoy solving problems and looking at things in new or different ways are ideal candidates for CTE. Check out the introductory programs that are offered in your area. Most high schools offer a wide variety of CTE programs, and even some middle schools have them.

By 2020, about 10 million new skilled workers will be needed in the United States alone. This huge demand means great opportunities for you!

DID YOU KNOW?

CTE professionals from many different career clusters work to help people before, during, and after a natural disaster occurs.

After a storm, road crews work to clear and repair streets.

In 2005, carpenters, electricians, and plumbers were needed to build homes, such as the one below, to replace those destroyed by Hurricane Katrina in New Orleans, Louisiana.

JOBS IN
HUMAN SERVICES

A career in human services allows you to help others. You can assist people who are learning to walk again after an accident or turn someone into an alien with carefully applied makeup.

Jobs in human services are for people who like people. Marketers want to know what needs people have and what products will help fill those needs. Career coaches give advice on what jobs will work best for specific individuals. Massage therapists help to relieve stress and reduce pain. There are so many exciting ways that you can make a real difference in people's lives.

HUMAN SERVICE JOB PATHWAYS:

EARLY CHILDHOOD DEVELOPMENT AND SERVICES	Workers assist children and young people as they grow and learn.
COUNSELING AND MENTAL HEALTH SERVICES	Professionals help young people and adults when they run into problems. The difficulties can be mental, emotional, or both mental and emotional.
FAMILY AND COMMUNITY SERVICES	Professionals coach individuals and families on how to get along with each other and the community. They also assist the ill and elderly.
PERSONAL CARE SERVICES	Workers make everyone look and feel their best.
CONSUMER SERVICES	Employees advise people on making wise decisions.

HOW TO USE THIS BOOK

Each two-page spread focuses on a specific career in the Human Services CTE cluster. For each career, you will find a detailed description of life on the job, advice on the best educational path to take (see right), and tips on what you can do right now to begin preparing for your dream career. Let's get started!

SECONDARY SCHOOL

This section lists the best subjects to take in high school.

POST-SECONDARY

Some jobs require an **apprenticeship** and **certification** while others require a college or university degree. This section gives you an idea of the best path to take after high school.

Nuns, ministers, priests, rabbis, and **imams** often work with young people on projects that benefit a community.

Real estate agents keep a close watch on local housing markets to help their clients find their dream home.

Mark Jenkins is a personal trainer who has coached singers, rappers, and comedians. Beyoncé is among his many clients.

Makeup artists can get special training in special effects makeup.

PRESCHOOL
TEACHER

You can help make a child's introduction to school a fun and positive experience.

A preschool teacher uses play to help young children develop social and learning skills that prepare them for school. Research shows that children who participate in preschool programs have better health, social skills, emotional maturity, and **cognitive development**. Interest in preschool continues to grow, so openings for preschool teachers will increase.

Building towers helps children develop counting and color recognition skills.

ON THE JOB

As a preschool teacher, you organize each day so that children have a combination of physical activity (such as arts and crafts, music, and field trips), rest, and playtime (such as games and outdoor play). You plan activities that help children develop language, motor, and social skills. To encourage participation, you focus on their interests and use these in forms of play that promote the development of basic color, shape, number, and letter recognition skills. You work both with groups of children and one-on-one, depending on individual needs. During all activities, you observe the stage of development of each child and identify any emotional or developmental problems. You keep records of each child's progress, routines, and interests, and bring both achievements and problems to the attention of parents and guardians.

WHAT CAN YOU DO NOW?

Take a babysitting course. To get experience with young children, find work as a babysitter or camp counselor. Alternatively, volunteer to help lead community programs for young children.

DID YOU KNOW?

Since 1965, Head Start programs in the United States have helped more than 34 million young children develop social, emotional, and early learning skills.

YOUR PATH TO WORK AS A PRESCHOOL TEACHER

SECONDARY SCHOOL

Math, art, physical education, computers, and science classes are a great start.

POST-SECONDARY

Early childhood education certification or a college degree is required.

Children build vocabulary, word recognition, and other pre-reading skills by listening to stories. By hearing the same story many times, they learn the rhythm of language.

Art programs, such as hand painting, encourage creativity and **fine motor skills**—and they are fun!

Group play helps children develop social skills.

TEACHER
ASSISTANT

Teacher assistants help classroom teachers by providing extra attention and instruction for students who need it.

Today's classrooms include children with special physical, mental, and language needs. There is a bright outlook for teacher assistants, because they are vital to helping these students succeed.

Students with hearing challenges may need assistance from someone who knows sign language.

This teacher assistant helps a student with a science experiment.

ON THE JOB

As a teacher assistant, you work hand in hand with a teacher to help students who need extra support. Sometimes you work with an individual student. More often, you work with a small group of children who are all experiencing similar difficulties. You focus on these students as you reinforce lessons taught by the classroom teacher. You also monitor how well they follow school and classroom rules and routines. Ahead of class, you help prepare teaching materials for each lesson and set up equipment. This often includes special materials for the children you assist, but may also involve the entire class. You assist with keeping records on each child's progress, attendance, and assessments. When needed, you supervise students during class time, lunch, and recess. You also lend a hand during field trips.

Some teacher assistants specialize in coaching students on computers.

YOUR PATH TO WORK AS A TEACHER ASSISTANT

SECONDARY SCHOOL

Math, art, language arts, computers, and a second language are advised.

POST-SECONDARY

Two years of college for teacher assistants is required.

DID YOU KNOW?

The Title 1 program is a U.S. government strategy that provides extra funding to educational agencies and schools that have a large number of low-income families. Teacher assistants who work in these programs must have a two-year degree or pass a state or local assessment.

WHAT CAN YOU DO NOW?

Volunteer to tutor peers or younger students. Look for the kinds of problems they have and brainstorm ways to help. Participate in school sports and clubs to experience working as a member of a team.

Many teacher assistants constantly upgrade their skills. Some go on to train as teachers.

ART THERAPIST

Art therapists plan and conduct art therapy sessions to help improve the physical and emotional well-being of their clients.

Openings for this exciting job are growing at a fast rate, as people come to understand how art can help those with physical and emotional challenges feel better about themselves and their lives.

ON THE JOB

As an art therapist, you plan and conduct sessions that allow clients to use art to express their experiences as they recover from or cope with mental, emotional, or physical issues. You work with clients as they draw or paint, sculpt, sew and work with fabric, or make masks. You talk with and listen to them during each session. You observe and record their reactions. For example, making a warrior mask might help a child deal with difficult **chemotherapy** treatments. You reflect on reactions like these, acknowledge client communication, and consider how you might use additional art therapy to further increase progress. Away from clients, you write treatment plans, **case summaries**, and progress reports.

WHAT CAN YOU DO NOW?

Learn about the different styles of art. Join an art or drama club. Attend a local youth center and volunteer to help with activities.

An art therapy program at the Homefront homeless shelter in Ewing, New Jersey, allowed Emily Lewis to vent bottled-up anger from her past and move on with her life. She won a full scholarship to the Parsons School for Design in New York City. After graduation, Emily became a professional photographer.

YOUR PATH TO WORK AS AN ART THERAPIST

SECONDARY SCHOOL

Art, computer science, languages, and math classes are a good start.

POST-SECONDARY

A college or university degree in education or art therapy is required. Courses in psychology are also recommended.

A client's choice of color may express something about an issue he or she is working through. To find out, art therapists encourage their clients to talk about their creations. Reds and blacks often express anger, such as in this piece of art.

This after-school program uses art therapy to help members deal with emotional issues such as bullying.

As members of the **baby boom generation** age, recreational therapists help them maintain a healthy and fun lifestyle.

MENTAL HEALTH
COUNSELOR

Mental health counselors work with groups and individuals to help them stay mentally and emotionally healthy.

Openings in this field are growing, as people come to recognize the importance of mental health. With counselling, many people can deal with issues affecting their well-being before problems become more serious.

DID YOU KNOW?

Four out of every 100 American children experience **post-traumatic stress disorder (PTSD)** during their lifetime.

ON THE JOB

You use interviews, observation, and tests to assess clients. You encourage them to express their feelings and discuss what is happening in their lives. You listen to their words and notice their **body language** to get a clear picture of their wellness. Clients may find it difficult to adjust to the loss of a parent, job, or spouse. You coach them in developing **coping strategies**, such as **assertiveness** training. You maintain private records related to client treatment. You also fill out government forms, **diagnostic** records, and progress notes.

Meditation helps these emergency responders in a PTSD support group.

WHAT CAN YOU DO NOW?

When talking with friends and family, be conscious of listening to understand them. Volunteer to help lead a school group or coach a sports team. Notice the effects of the encouragement you give.

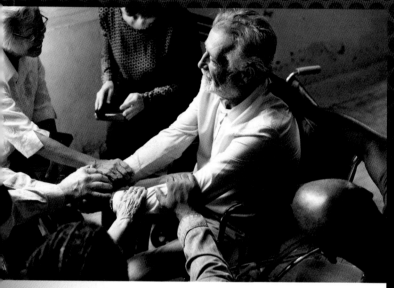

One out of four seniors lives with a mental health problem. Counselling can help them deal with the physical and mental effects of aging, such as memory loss and anxiety.

YOUR PATH TO WORK AS A MENTAL HEALTH COUNSELLOR

SECONDARY SCHOOL

Math, computer science, history, languages, and sociology are recommended.

POST-SECONDARY

A college or university degree in psychology or a related field, as well as licensing, is required.

DID YOU KNOW?

Most people at some point in their lives experience emotional difficulty or pain. If you do, it is important to talk about it with a trusted adult or counsellor. Never feel ashamed to ask for help or talk about your feelings.

This counsellor is leading a session on eating disorders and healthy **body image**.

PHYSICAL
THERAPIST ASSISTANT

ysical therapist assistants support physical therapists who
k with injured clients to help them improve their mobility.

Job openings in this field are
expected to grow by at least 40
percent by 2020 due to increased
interest in fitness and aging baby
boomers. Fitness buffs tend to have
more sports injuries. As people age,
they need help to deal with age-
related conditions, such as arthritis.

ON THE JOB

As a physical therapist assistant,
you work as a member of a team
that includes at least one physical
therapist. You provide hands-on
physical therapy to clients. Clients
include people who have some type of
condition that limits their movement.
This could result from a condition
such as **spina bifida**, a car accident,
or simply aging. You assist clients in
regaining mobility using treatments
that include exercise, massage, and
both **electrotherapy** and **ultrasound**
equipment. You make sure that clients
are safe and comfortable during each
treatment. You record the results and
discuss follow-up with the physical
therapist in charge of each case.

People who have lost a limb
need special training in learning
how to use a **prosthesis**.
This includes work on strength,
coordination, and endurance.

Physical therapy
assistants help
clients do exercises
that improve their
physical abilities.

WHAT CAN YOU DO NOW?

Focus on classes in health and physical education so that you become aware of the body's muscle groups and how they are affected by sports and injuries.

DID YOU KNOW?

Each year, more than one million people around the world have a limb amputated. That's one every 30 seconds.

YOUR PATH TO WORK AS A PHYSICAL THERAPIST ASSISTANT

SECONDARY SCHOOL

Good courses to take are health, physical education, math, sociology, and computer science.

POST-SECONDARY

Most colleges have physical therapist assistant programs.

People can lose mobility due to **neurological** damage resulting from a head injury, stroke, or other disease, such as cancer. With determination and physical therapy, many can learn to walk again.

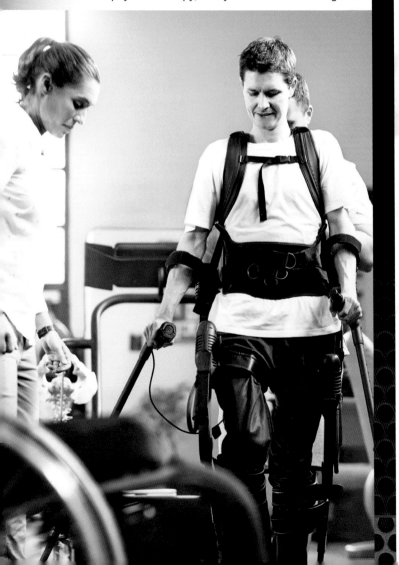

Sick and injured patients may have difficulty moving from their bed to a wheelchair or from a wheelchair to a toilet. Physical therapist assistants can teach them how to do this safely.

CHILD AND YOUTH
WORKER

Child and youth workers provide programming that helps young people feel good about themselves and keeps them out of trouble.

Many forces add stress to the lives of today's teens. These include the demands of family, friends, and school, as well as the ongoing pressure caused by social media.

ON THE JOB

As a child and youth worker, you interact with young people and their families to help them develop safe and positive relationships. This includes developing personal relationships with young people and providing a positive role model. You supervise and manage youth groups, as well as organize, plan, and implement social and recreational activities. In your interactions with youth, you try to encourage their self-esteem and help them develop positive behaviors. You acquire information about **resources** available in the community and provide contacts to clients when needed. Depending on a client's needs and interests, you may also provide housing support or **dietary** coaching.

Listening to a teen talk about a traumatic experience may identify the need for ongoing social or mental health support.

DID YOU KNOW?

Sacred Circle is a ME to WE program that encourages **Indigenous** youth to be leaders in their communities. The program focuses on confidence building, academic achievement, community building, and celebration of cultural identity.

Low self-esteem in youth leads to higher school dropout rates. At a self-esteem-building workshop, these teens are learning how to build confidence and have fun.

WHAT CAN YOU DO NOW?

Volunteer to work at an after-school program or drop-in center. Learn about issues or problems that young people in other communities are dealing with. Practice active listening as others share their stories with you.

YOUR PATH TO WORK AS A CHILD AND YOUTH WORKER

SECONDARY SCHOOL

Math, science, physical education, languages, computer science, and history are good choices.

POST-SECONDARY

A college degree in child and youth care is required.

A youth worker gathers information about the legal issues a client is facing.

Youth workers can help parents understand and deal with inappropriate child behavior.

ESTHETICIAN

Estheticians help people feel good about themselves by assisting them in looking their best. This includes working on skin, hair, and nails.

People who look good feel good about themselves. Working on that principle, estheticians coach young people in ways to highlight their best looks. They also assist older clients in minimizing the wrinkles and skin problems that accompany aging.

DID YOU KNOW?

Behind every celebrity's good looks is a top esthetician like Florida's Tammy Fender. Tammy believes that beauty happens from the inside out. She advises clients to eat healthy foods. Her sessions include facial treatments with **reflexology**, a form of massage used to relieve stress and treat illness.

ON THE JOB

As an esthetician, you work on a client's face and body. You provide facial treatments that address skin concerns, such as acne. You give face and scalp massages that help relax muscles and reduce stress. You also offer sugar and salt scrubs that remove dead skin. In addition, you use **electrolysis**, waxing, and other techniques to remove unwanted body hair. You take time to analyze the features of a client's face and then do makeovers. This involves using makeup to highlight good points while hiding problem areas, such as redness. You clean and refresh the treatment room after each treatment. You also record notes from client treatments, which you can refer to at the client's next appointment.

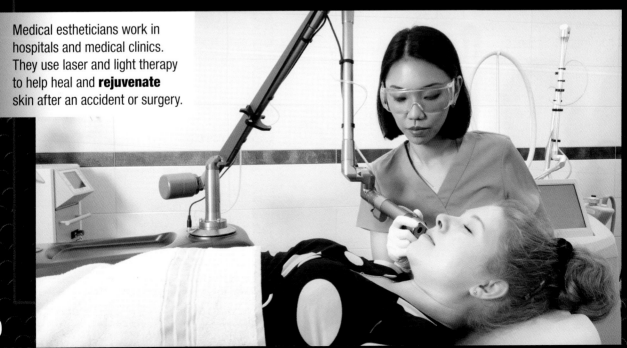

Medical estheticians work in hospitals and medical clinics. They use laser and light therapy to help heal and **rejuvenate** skin after an accident or surgery.

WHAT CAN YOU DO NOW?

Volunteer with your school drama club or a local drama society. Offer to assist with the makeup. Learn everything you can about different kinds of makeup and hair styling techniques. Check out online tutorials to learn some new looks.

Many people hire an esthetician to do their makeup for special occasions.

YOUR PATH TO WORK AS AN ESTHETICIAN

SECONDARY SCHOOL

Business, math, marketing, languages, and CTE classes in cosmetology, if available, are great choices.

POST-SECONDARY

Requirements differ depending on where you live. Most expect a college diploma and licence.

An esthetician removes unwanted facial hair from this client's eyebrows, upper lip, and chin.

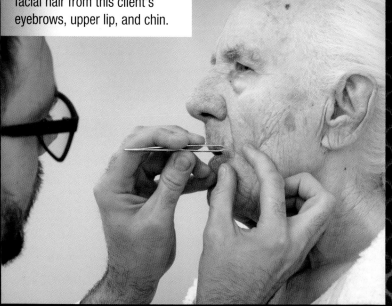

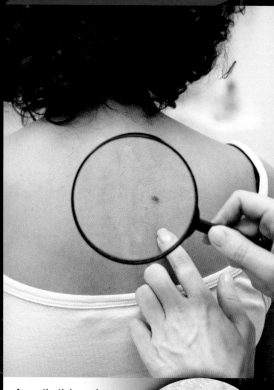

An esthetician who spots an unusual growth on a client's skin may refer the person to a doctor. The growth could be an early sign of cancer.

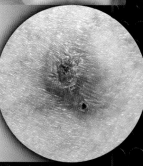

FUNERAL
ATTENDANT

Funeral attendants do many tasks to make things easier for people who have lost a loved one.

Funeral attendants greet mourners as they arrive for a funeral.

Funeral attendants fill out death certificates, get **permits**, write or edit **obituaries**, and post online information about upcoming funerals and memorial services.

It's extremely difficult to deal with the death of someone we love. Having funeral attendants who care about people makes things a little easier. Openings for these jobs may increase slightly as the population ages, especially for those willing to appreciate the funeral practices of other cultures.

ON THE JOB

Your role as funeral attendant starts immediately after a death, when you transport the body to a funeral home. You assist the funeral director in preparing both the corpse and a parlor or chapel for a funeral. This includes **embalming** the corpse. You also apply makeup to help make the corpse look similar to the way the person did in life. You place the casket in the funeral parlor or chapel prior to any service. Depending on what is wanted, you arrange flowers or lights around the casket, direct or escort mourners, and close the casket at the end of any viewing. After each service, you store funeral equipment for future use.

WHAT CAN YOU DO NOW?

Join a speech or debate club to develop your communication skills. Ask if you can tour a funeral home in your area. Learn about the funeral practices of different cultures.

Many people plan and pay for their funeral years ahead of their death.

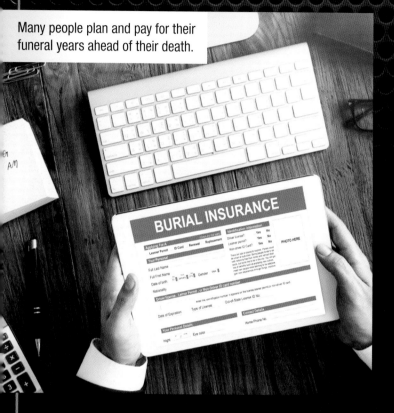

YOUR PATH TO WORK AS A FUNERAL ATTENDANT

SECONDARY SCHOOL

Focus on languages, biology, chemistry, business, math, marketing, and computers.

POST-SECONDARY

College programs are available in **mortuary science**. Requirements differ depending on where you live.

DID YOU KNOW?

The Day of the Dead is a holiday in Mexico that begins every year on October 31. People go to cemeteries to honor and celebrate the memory of their deceased loved ones. Family and friends place gifts and photos and even the deceased person's favorite food or snacks beside their grave.

Coffins come in a wide variety of styles. There are even **eco-friendly** wicker coffins woven from willow, sea grass, or bamboo.

IN-HOME
HEALTH AIDE

...ne health aides provide routine
...lth care that can be done outside
...ospital setting.

...n 2012, less than 14 percent of the American
...oopulation was 65 and older. By 2029, this
...oercentage is expected to climb to around
...20 percent. As a result, more citizens will
...need workers who can help them continue
...to live independently in their own home.

ON THE JOB

...You assist clients by providing routine care,
...such as bathing, dressing, changing bandages,
...and giving medications. You help those with
...mobility problems as they move in and out of
...beds, baths, and wheelchairs. You change
...their bedding and wash and iron laundry.
...n some cases, you shop for groceries and
...orepare well-balanced meals. You keep
...clients socially and mentally alert by talking
...with and reading to them. You encourage
...them to exercise and/or participate in
...community activities. You keep records of
...the care you provide, your client's condition
...and progress, as well as any difficulties.

WHAT CAN YOU DO NOW?

...Volunteer at a seniors' or group home.
...Visit with clients, listen to their stories,
...and perform small tasks for them.

Home health care is a cost-effective practice
that allows people to maintain healthy social
relationships with members of their community.

With the assistance of someone who can help her dress
and replace her sling, this client can care for herself at home

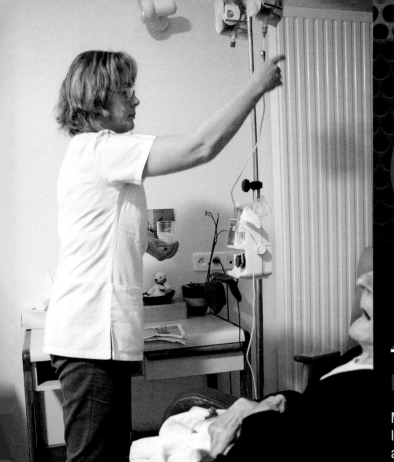

YOUR PATH TO WORK AS A HOME HEALTH AIDE

SECONDARY SCHOOL

Social sciences, math, languages, physical education, marketing, and computer science are helpful courses.

POST-SECONDARY

Certification is required. First aid and food safety training is also highly recommended.

This aide is replacing the feeding tube for a client with **ALS**, a condition that affects the ability to swallow.

DID YOU KNOW?

Many Americans aged 75 and older have at least one **chronic** medical condition, such as asthma or heart disease. Care that keeps patients in their homes instead of a hospital saves hundreds of dollars per day and is also more comfortable for the patients.

This aide and her client leave a group home to attend a community concert.

CREDIT
COUNSELOR

Credit counselors advise and educate individuals and organizations about how to manage their debt.

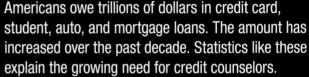

This credit counselor meets with clients to gather information about their current financial status.

One way to get a good credit rating is to apply for a credit card and pay off your purchases on a monthly basis.

Americans owe trillions of dollars in credit card, student, auto, and mortgage loans. The amount has increased over the past decade. Statistics like these explain the growing need for credit counselors.

ON THE JOB

Your job as a credit counselor includes interviewing clients about their finances. You ask for their current income, assets, debts, expenses, and credit rating. Using this data, you help them create a budget that will allow them to pay off any debts. You review the kinds of loans available and discuss the advantages and restrictions of each. You may suggest clients **consolidate** what they owe into one large loan with a lower **interest rate**. If they make too little to pay off their debts, you may advise them to declare **bankruptcy**. For others, you suggest useful investments that will help them prepare for future expenses and for retirement.

DID YOU KNOW?

The United States and Canada have different Financial Literacy Months—November in Canada and April in the United States. Throughout the year, the Council for Economic Education trains teachers to help students learn more about finances and how to handle money.

WHAT CAN YOU DO NOW?

Try playing a financial simulation game, such as Papa's Cupcakeria from learn4good.com. Set a monthly budget for yourself that includes spending, saving, and giving to charity.

YOUR PATH TO WORK AS A CREDIT COUNSELLOR

SECONDARY SCHOOL

Important subjects to study are math, computer science, and business.

POST-SECONDARY

A college or university degree in commerce or finance is usually required.

Borrowing money on your credit card or from pay day loan companies is very expensive. It is wiser to wait until you can pay cash for items.

Some credit counselors offer debt management courses that prevent people from needing their services in the future.

SPECIAL EVENTS
COORDINATOR

Special events coordinators plan meetings, conventions, weddings, and other special events.

Between 2008 and 2018, this field grew by 16 percent and is expected to grow by another 10 percent. This is because hiring a professional saves time and money. Successful events are also good publicity for **sponsoring** corporations.

ON THE JOB

This is the job for you if you like variety, are well organized, have a creative flair, and thrive on change. Be prepared to work long hours and weekends. You start the day handling e-mail and social media. You follow up with clients and respond to new leads. You study the **venues**, menus, and cool ideas in the latest event news. During client meetings, you discuss the timing, location, and budget for their event. Later, you work to coordinate accommodation, transportation, and food. That means visiting possible venues, talking to chefs and caterers, checking out audiovisual suppliers, and negotiating for good pric es. Although finalizing everything might take weeks, your main job starts during the event, when you are on hand 24/7 to troubleshoot any problems. When the impossible occurs, it is your job to fix it.

The volunteers, performers, and advertising for this **powwow** were coordinated by members of the Kahnawake Mohawk Nation.

WHAT CAN YOU DO NOW?

Plan a party for family or friends and make a detailed list of every step you will need to take to make the party a success. Volunteer to help plan an event at your school.

DID YOU KNOW?

Networking is a method of developing business contacts by interacting with others to exchange information. It is a great marketing tool and a good way to develop a list of dependable **vendors**.

YOUR PATH TO WORK AS A SPECIAL EVENTS COORDINATOR

SECONDARY SCHOOL

Marketing, drama, languages, math, and business courses are highly recommended.

POST-SECONDARY

Colleges offer programs in event planning. Certification for the specific type of planner you want to be, such as a wedding planner, is required.

Many convention centers, hotels, and stadiums have coordinators on staff.

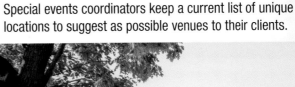

Special events coordinators keep a current list of unique locations to suggest as possible venues to their clients.

When a hurricane knocked out the power for a large press event, the coordinator organized a candlelight presentation that impressed both the clients and attending journalists.

A use of technology helps to make an event memorable.

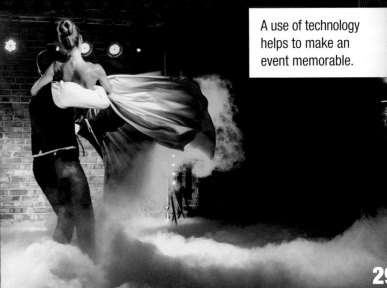

LEARNING MORE

BOOKS

Christen, Carol and Richard N. Bolles. *What Color Is Your Parachute? for Teens, Third Edition: Discover Yourself, Design Your Future, and Plan for Your Dream Job.* Ten Speed Press, 2015.

Kindersley, Dorling. *The Careers Handbook: The Graphic Guide to Finding the Perfect Job for You.* Dorling Kindersley Limited, 2015.

WEBSITES

WWW.BLS.GOV/OOH	United States Department of Labor Occupational Outlook	On this site you will find valuable information on a wide variety of jobs.
HTTP://NOC.ESDC.GC.CA/ ENGLISH/NOC/WELCOME. ASPX?VER=16	Government of Canada	Enter the name of the job that interests you. The site will link you to the main duties and employment requirements for this job, as well as a list of similar professions.
WWW.MYNEXTMOVE.ORG/ EXPLORE/IP	My Next Move	Find out what your interests are and how they might lead to a career.
HTTP://MAPPINGYOURFUTURE. ORG/PLANYOURCAREER/ CAREERSHIP/INDEX.CFM	CareerShip	Match your interests to possible careers and find out more about each one.

GLOSSARY

ALS Also called Lou Gehrig's disease. A condition that stops the brain from communicating with the rest of the body, resulting in gradual paralysis.

apprenticeship A period of time spent learning skilled work with hands-on training

assertiveness Confident behavior that allows people to ask for what they want or need

baby boom generation A large group of people born between 1946 and 1964

bankruptcy When someone is unable to pay their debts

body image How a person views their own appearance

body language Communicating through body positions and movements

case summary A brief description of clients and the problems they are facing

certification Certificate that shows someone has achieved a certain level of skill and knowledge

chemotherapy Treatment of cancer by chemicals intended to kill the abnormal cells

chronic Persistent or recurring

cognitive development Level of skill in processing information and learning language

consolidate To join various things together

coping strategy A successful way to deal with a problem

diagnostic Concerned with assessing the level of an illness or health problem

dietary Related to food

eco-friendly Safe for the environment

electrolysis Removal of hair roots or small blemishes using an electric current

electrotherapy Use of an electric current to stimulate nerves and muscles

embalming Preserving a dead body from decay by injecting preservatives into the corpse

fine motor skills Ability to use fingers and hands for tasks

imam A person who leads prayer in a mosque

Indigenous Original occupant of a land

interest rate Amount a borrower pays in exchange for a loan

meditation A time for quiet thought

mortuary science The study of funeral practices

Mount Everest The highest mountain in the world, located in Asia

neurological Relating to the nerves and nervous system, including the brain

obituary A notice of death that includes a brief biography of the deceased

permit Written legal permission

post-traumatic stress disorder (PTSD) Ongoing mental and emotional stress brought on by a severe psychological shock

powwow An Indigenous ceremony which includes feasting and dancing

prosthesis Artificial body part such as a false leg or arm

pyrotechnics The art of making and displaying fireworks

reflexology Applying pressure to hands or feet to ease tension in the body

rejuvenate To make healthy again

resources Sources of aid available for use

spina bifida A defect of the spine in which part of the spinal cord is exposed

sponsor A business that pays for a program or event in order to gain publicity

ultrasound The use of sound or other vibrations to obtain a digital image

vendor A person or company offering something for sale

venue A place where an event, such as a conference or performance, occurs

INDEX

apprenticeship 7

baby boom generation
   13, 16
body image 15
body language 14
bullying 13

career clusters 4, 5, 7
certification 7, 9, 25, 29
cognitive development
   8
coping strategies 12,
   14, 18
Council for Economic
   Education 26
counselling 12–13,
   14–15, 18–19,
   26–27
credit rating 26

Day of the Dead 23

electrolysis 20

Fender, Tammy 20
Financial Literacy
   Month 26

Jenkins, Mark 7
job pathways 4, 6

Head Start 9
Homefront 12
Hurricane Katrina 5

Kahnawake Mohawk
   Nation 28

Lewis, Emily 12

makeup 6, 7, 20, 21
meditation 14
mental health 14–15,
   18
ME to WE 18
Mount Everest 5

networking 29

Papa's Cupcakeria 27
Parsons School for
   Design 12
pay day loans 27
post-traumatic stress
   disorder (PTSD) 14
powwow 28
prosthesis 16

reflexology 20

Sacred Circle 18
self-esteem 6, 12–13,
   14–15, 18–19, 20
sign language 10
skills 4, 8, 9, 11, 14, 23

Title 1 11

venue 28, 29